W9-BUO-177

Dennis the Menace

SUPERCHARGED and EVER READY!

By HANK KETCHAM

FAWCETT GOLD MEDAL • NEW YORK

A Fawcett Gold Medal Book
Published by Ballantine Books

Library of Congress Catalog Card Number: 82-190861

ISBN 0-449-12391-X

Manufactured in the United States of America

First Ballantine Books Edition: March 1983

ABOUT THE AUTHOR

HANK KETCHAM has been drawing the adventures of DENNIS THE MENACE for 32 years, 18 of which were produced in Switzerland. The spunky half pint appears daily and Sunday in 850 newspapers, in 48 different countries and in 14 languages. Hank recently repatriated and currently lives in California midst a cluster of golf courses.

"MR. WILSON SAYS SOMEDAY OUR TUB IS GONNA BE KNOWN AS THE BATHTUB THAT ATE MAPLE STREET."

"I UNDERSTAND LITTLE BOYS BECAUSE I HAVE TWO *GRANDSONS*."

"I GOT TWO *GRANDMAS*, BUT I DON'T UNDERSTAND OLD LADIES!"

"YOU KNOW WHAT I THINK? I THINK GETTIN' DIRTY IS **GOOD** FOR A PERSON!"

"JOEY'S GOT A PENNY, TOMMY'S GOT A NICKEL AN' I GOT A DIME! HOW MANY BANANA SPLITS IS THAT?"

"....I LIVE NEXT DOOR. MY NAME IS DENNIS. UH HUH. WHO? OH, SURE. HE'S HERE. IT'S FOR *YOU*, MR. WILSON."

" WELL, I'LL BE DARNED! DENNIS AND MR. WILSON ARE
PLAYING TAG!...OR IS WILSON TRYING TO...?"

"I'M GONNA LEND YA MY LIGHTNING BUGS. THEN YOU'LL **NEVER** HAVE TO SLEEP IN THE DARK."

"FIFTY-FIVE YEARS OLD?! BOY, YOU BETTER **SIT DOWN**!"

"RUFF'S A *PRIVATE DETECTIVE* DOG. THAT'S LIKE A POLICE DOG, ONLY NOBODY KNOWS IT."

"NO ONE HERE CAN LOVE OR UNDERSTAND ME..."

"ALL RIGHT! YOUR FIVE MINUTES ARE UP."

"CAN WE AFFORD A BROTHER IF I CAN RENT HIM FOR A DIME A DAY?"

"WHAT ARE YA *DOIN'*, MARGARET? DON'T YOU KNOW THIS IS A **ONE-WAY** STREET?"

"HEY, DAD! THEY SAID THEY **AREN'T** BUMS!"

"BUT YOU TOLD MRS. WILSON YOU WISHED SOMEBODY WOULD EAT 'EM BEFORE **YOU** DID!"

"MY DOG COULD WIN PRIZES, TOO, IF I WANTED TO **DRESS** HIM LIKE THAT!"

"GOT ANYTHING YOU WANT **SHORTER**?"

"GEE WHIZ, WHY GET SO MAD? I **SAID** I'D PAY FOR IT!"

"...AN' GOD BLESS MOM, EVEN IF SHE HASN'T MADE ANY COOKIES IN ABOUT TWO YEARS."

"IT'S A **MOLE**...WHAT ON EARTH MADE YOU THINK IT WAS A KANGAROO?"

"THEY LIVE DOWN THERE SOMEPLACE."

"MAYBE I DON'T GET IT FROM *ANYBODY*...
MAYBE I'M THE FIRST OF MY KIND."

"SOON AS YOU LEARN TO READ, JOEY, THE WHOLE WORLD'S AGAINST YOU."

"TELL US AGAIN ABOUT NICKEL CANDY BARS, MR. WILSON."

"I DON'T EVEN WANTA *LOOK* AT ANYTHING CALLED SQUASH!"

"HOW SORRY CAN YA BE FOR BUSTIN' ONE LOUSY DISH?"

"DON'T SAY TOMBOY, SAY TOM-**GIRL**...UNLESS YOU WANTA GET **CLOBBERED**."

"THIS IS GONNA BE ONE OF MY **GOOD** DAYS. I GOT AWAY WITH THREE THINGS ALREADY AN' IT'S ONLY TEN O'CLOCK."

"I THINK THAT WAS THE BORINGEST MORNING YOU EVER MADE ME HAVE!"

"YOU GUYS HIDE AROUND THE YARD. I'LL LET YOU IN ONE-AT-A-TIME SO MY MOM WON'T GET SO EXCITED."

" OH, NO! "

"THE BIGGEST CARROT CROP IN TEN YEARS."

"YOU SAID YOU DIDN'T HAVE *TIME* TO FIX MY SCOOTER.
YOU CALL **THAT** BEIN' BUSY?"

"NO MATTER **WHAT** HE SAYS, DEAR, GEORGE LOVES YOU..."

"**REALLY**, GEORGE?"

" I DON'T THINK HE'S GONNA SETTLE FOR MILK...HE SOUNDS
LIKE HE WANTS A **HAMBURGER**!"

"LOOK, JOEY! GOD'S GOT HIS **COLORIN'** SET OUT!"

"YOU SEE? IT JUST **SEEMS** LIKE HE NEVER SLEEPS."

"YEAH, SHE'S GOT A **LOT** OF KNIVES. SHE'S PART **PIRATE**!"

"GEE, I DIDN'T KNOW ANY OF 'EM FLY AT **NIGHT**!
I BETTER FILL MR. WILSON'S BIRD BATH!"

"I DON'T **LIKE** GETTIN' HAIRCUTS FROM PEOPLE THAT CAN SEND ME TO BED!"

"SURE IS FUNNY THAT WE'D **BOTH** GET HUNGRY FOR PEANUT BUTTER SAMWICHES AT THE SAME TIME!"

"I BEEN WATCHIN' YA SLEEP. YOU WERE GOIN' PSSSSSS...AND MOM WAS GOIN' BZZZZZZ!"

'MOM! DID YOU KNOW *THESE* ARE GROWIN' AGAIN?"

"I'M COMING OUT OF RETIREMENT. I'VE BEEN OFFERED TWO CENTS EACH FOR EVERY LIZARD I CAN CATCH."

"YA BIG SISSY!"

"PENNY FOR YOUR THOUGHTS."

"WE GOT SOME THOUGHTS FOR SALE!"

"WHAT'S WRONG WITH THIS DARN OL' ORANGE JUICE?"

"IT'S GRAPEFRUIT JUICE."

"GEE, I GUESS I NEVER SEEN YA BEFORE WITHOUT YOUR GLASSES, MRS. WILSON!"

"GREAT PARTY, MARGARET. I HOPE YOUR MOM'S NERVISS BREAKDOWN IS BETTER BY TOMORROW."

"WHAT'S BEIN' 'TOO BIG FOR MY BRITCHES' GOT TO DO WITH ME HAVING TO SIT IN THIS CORNER ?"

"DENNIS PHONED AND SAID TO TELL YOU NOT TO WORRY. THAT NO MATTER WHAT EVERYONE ELSE SAYS, HE DIDN'T DO IT."

"I KNOW I'M LATE, BUT A BIRD WAS SINGING TO ME
AN' IT WASN'T POLITE TO LEAVE BEFORE HE FINISHED."

"I READ A BOOK ONCE ... BUT IT HARDLY
SEEMED WORTH DOIN'."

"IF I **HAD** A KITE, I'D GO FLY IT, MR. WILSON.
HOW ABOUT *MAKIN'* ME ONE?"

"YOU GOT A BIG **BEE** IN THERE, MARGARET!"

"HAPPY MOTHER'S DAY, MOM!"

" IF YOU ORDER FROG LEGS, I'M **LEAVIN'**!"

"AW, IT'S OKAY, I GUESS. BUT WHY CAN'T WE EVER EAT AT A **DRIVE-IN**?"

"TURNIPS... SPINACH... CARROTS! BOY, YOU'RE REALLY MAD AT THE WORLD TODAY, AREN'TCHA?"

"YES, IT LOOKS EXACTLY LIKE A LITTLE NAKED BOY.
NOW DRAW SOMETHING ELSE!"

"WE'LL ALL BE COMIN' TO YOUR HOUSE TOMORROW...'SPECIALLY
IF IT RAINS AND THEY CLOSE THE GOLF COURSE."

"DENNIS!"

"SHHHHH... ISN'T THAT THE
HAPPIEST BUNCH OF FROGS
YA EVER HEARD?"

"I'M **NOT** FEEDIN' THE WHOLE NEIGHBORHOOD! JUST THEIR KIDS."

"SEE IF THEY HAVE ANY OF THAT KITTY FOOD CALLED 'ROWWR'. HE ASKS FOR IT ALL THE TIME."

"NOW I KNOW HOW THOSE GUYS ON THE 'WANTED' POSTERS FEEL!"

"THE PLUMBER SAYS IT'S THE ONLY HUNDRED-DOLLAR YO-YO IN TOWN."

"WHEN YOU GONNA WRAP HER AROUND YOUR LITTLE FINGER?"

"GET *LOST*, WILL YA, JOEY?!"

"DON'T WORRY ABOUT RUININ' MY NEW SHOES, MOM...
I LEFT 'EM SOMEWHERE."

"YOU SURE KNOW HOW TO MAKE A PERSON FEEL RIGHT AT **HOME**, MR. WILSON!"

"ARRGH!"

"HI, MR. WILSON...WHAT ELSE IS NEW?"

"MR. WILSON IS GONNA CLEAN OUT HIS GARAGE. I BETTER GO HELP HIM."

"HE STARTED WITH ME!"

"IT'S NOT **SAFE** TO WALK THE STREETS IN THIS NEIGHBORHOOD NO MORE! I RAN INTO MARGARET THREE TIMES TODAY!"

"WHY DO YOU ALWAYS WANT TO SIT ON MY LAP?"

"BECAUSE IT'S **THERE** . . . SOMEPLACE."

"HE'S GOT A LOT OF **EVERYTHING** IN HIM."

"WHY DON'T YOU SURPRISE US SOMETIME WITH **TWO** KINDS OF DESSERT AN' ONLY **ONE** VEG'TABLE?"

"I *ALWAYS* HAVE TROUBLE WITH THOSE THINGS!
WHY DON'T THEY MAKE **SQUARE** PEAS?"

"THE BAKERY STUFF? OH, I FINISHED
IT AND THREW THE BAG AWAY, WHY?"

"WHO LICKS YOUR BOWLS?"

"ARE YOU GONNA BELIEVE YOUR OWN EYES, OR ARE YA GONNA BELIEVE ME?"

"DUMB QUESTION."

"ABOUT THIS AFTERNOON ... IF YOU'LL TAKE A LOOK AT THE INSTANT REPLAY, YOU'LL SEE IT WASN'T ALL MY FAULT."

"I GET SO DIRTY BECAUSE I'M CLOSER
TO WHERE THE DIRT **IS**!"

"WHAT DO YOU MEAN, 'THE CRUMMY OLD COOKIE JAR WE **USED** TO HAVE'?"

"MR. WILSON **NEVER** EXERCISES! EITHER HE'S CHASIN' SOMETHING OR SOMETHING'S CHASIN' **HIM**!"

"GO HOME!"   "HE FORGOT TO SAY, 'YANKEE'."

"YOUR MOTHER HAS A MIND OF HER OWN, SON."

"DOES THAT MEAN YOURS IS *BORROWED*?"

"SEEMS LIKE OLD TIMES...YOU OUT THERE AND ME IN HERE."

"YUK! THAT WAS THE LOUSIEST SODA POP I EVER TASTED!"

"HEY! WHO DRANK MY BEER?"

"YOU'RE S'POSED TO GIVE ME 'TIL *SUNDOWN* TO GET OUT OF YOUR YARD, MR. WILSON!"

"WHEN I KICK YOU IN THE RIBS, YOU'RE S'POSED TO GALLOP."

"WELL, IT SURE LOOKS LIKE THE YEAR OF THE CHILD IS OVER!"

"GOSH, GINA... YOUR MOM'S SOUP IS LIKE WHAT WE CALL DINNER AT OUR HOUSE!"

"CAN'T YA FEEL IT, JOEY? EVERYTHING IS JUST **ITCHIN'**
TO PUSH UP OUT OF THE GROUND AND LOOK PRETTY!"

"YEAH? GEE, I THOUGHT A RAZZBERRY WAS A **NOISE** !"

" I CAN'T SLEEP. WANNA PLAY CATCH ? "

"IT MAY BE SPRING IN THE AIR, BUT IT'S STILL **WINTER** IN THOSE CEMENT STEPS!"

"YOU'RE NOT GONNA LET A COUPLA POUNDS STAND BETWEEN US AND A CHOCKLIT CAKE, ARE YOU?"

"YOU SHOULDA SAID 'GOOD KITTY' WHEN HE BROUGHT IN THE MOUSE...NOT 'YECHH'!"

"TALK ABOUT MIRACLES...YOU SHOULDA **SEEN** THIS PLACE WHEN WE SPOTTED YOU COMIN' UP THE WALK!"

"YOU SENT US A PRETTY GOOD WINTER... BUT NOW I'M READY FOR SPRING ANY TIME **YOU** ARE."

"I THINK YOU'RE IN FOR IT. MOM SAID,
'JUST WAIT UNTIL YOUR FATHER COMES HOME'."

"I DIDN'T MEAN TO EAT IT ALL UP...BUT THE PART THAT WAS LEFT KEPT GETTIN' SMALLER AN' SMALLER, TILL IT WAS HARDLY WORTH SAVIN'."

"WHY DON'T YOU JUST CHANGE MY NAME TO *LITTLE JACK HORNER?*"

"SURE, I WAS HOLDIN' HANDS WITH GINA ... WHEN SHE GETS MAD, YOU **BETTER** BE HOLDIN' HER HANDS!"

"I CAN'T HARDLY HEAR YA...MY EARS ARE STILL RINGIN' FROM MR. WILSON."

"SEE? THAT'S WHAT I BEEN TRYIN' TO TELL YA ...
IT **HURTS** TO GET SOAP IN YOUR EYES!"

"PAPER ISN'T REALLY MY THING...
I DO MY BEST WORK ON **WALLS**."

"WANTA HEAR A GOOD ONE? THAT QUARTER YOU GAVE
ME TURNED OUT TO BE A DOLLAR!"

"I ATE THERE ONCE. THEY PUT PIECES O' *NEWSPAPER* IN THEIR COOKIES."

"ONLY CHILD HE MAY BE... LONELY HE'S **NOT** !"

"HEY, WE GOTTA GO BACK! I LEFT MY SHOES 'N SOCKS NEXT TO THEIR BEARSKIN RUG!"

"WELL, AMEN TILL NEXT WEEK, REV'REND POLITZER."

"JUST LEAVE YOUR HEAD AN' WE'LL COME BACK FOR IT LATER."

"HEY, JOEY! I WAS ONLY **KIDDING**!"

"LOOK, I'LL SHOW YA AGAIN. FIRST YA FOLD ALL THE MEAT ON ONE SIDE, THEN YA TEAR THE SAMWICH IN HALF. *THEN* YA GIVE THE KID THE HALF WITH NO MEAT! GOT IT?"

"IT'S TOO COLD TO PLAY OUTDOORS, DEWEY. WHY DON'T YOU
ROUND UP ALL THE GUYS AN' COME OVER TO MY HOUSE!"

"I DON'T KNOW WHERE YOU *PUT* IT."

"WATCH."

"NAW, I DON'T WANNA MEET YOUR SISTER...THERE'S TOO MANY WIMMEN IN MY LIFE *NOW!*"

"NOBODY EVER **SAID** 'DON'T PAINT THE TOILET PURPLE'!"

"He's HYPHENATIN' TILL SPRING, JOEY... ALL YOU HAVTA DO IS DUST HIM ONCE IN AWHILE."

"I WAS JUST WONDERIN'... DID YOU EVER
FIND ALL YOUR MARBLES?"

"I DON'T MIND TALKIN' TO MARGARET... I SAID I DON'T WANNA **LISTEN** TO HER!"

"SOMETIMES IT'S ME, BUT MOSTLY HE JUST GETS UP ON THE WRONG SIDE OF THE BED."

"MAYBE YOU BETTER TAKE MY PICTURE SO YOU'LL KNOW WHAT I WAS WEARIN' WHEN LAST SEEN."

"HOW ABOUT A BIG KISS FOR VALENTINE'S DAY?"

"OKAY, BUT DON'T TELL NOBODY OR THEY'LL **ALL** WANT ONE."

"HOW DO YA SPELL 'GOOFY'?"

"YA KNOW WHAT SOMEBODY OUGHTA INVENT ?... UNBREAKABLE EGGS!"

"MAYBE IT DON'T *LOOK* LIKE IT, BUT I BEEN TEACHIN' A KID SOME *MANNERS*!"